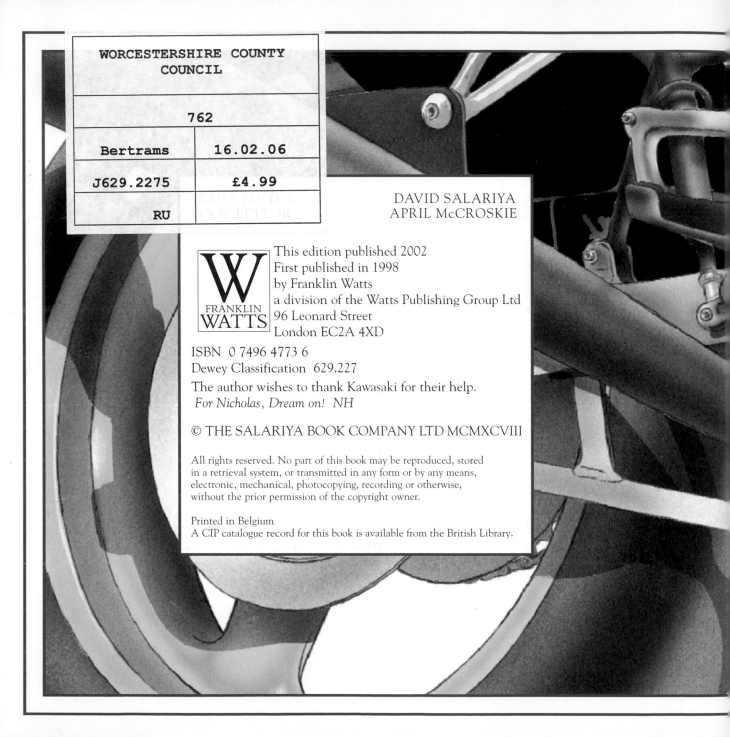

DAVID SALARIYA
APRIL McCROSKIE

FRANKLIN WATTS

This edition published 2002
First published in 1998
by Franklin Watts
a division of the Watts Publishing Group Ltd
96 Leonard Street
London EC2A 4XD

ISBN 0 7496 4773 6

Dewey Classification 629.227

The author wishes to thank Kawasaki for their help.
For Nicholas, Dream on! NH

© THE SALARIYA BOOK COMPANY LTD MCMXCVIII

Printed in Belgium
A CIP catalogue record for this book is available from the British Library.

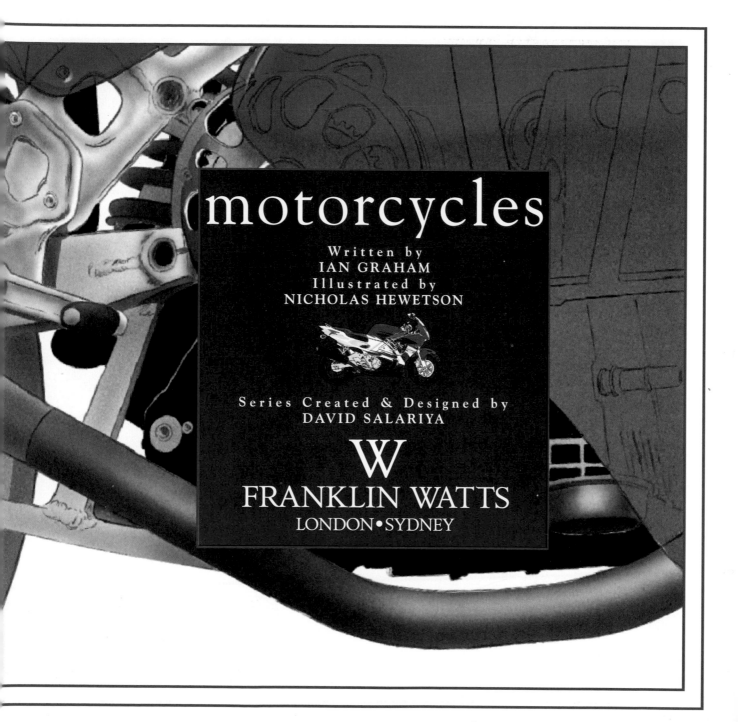

motorcycles

Written by
IAN GRAHAM
Illustrated by
NICHOLAS HEWETSON

Series Created & Designed by
DAVID SALARIYA

W
FRANKLIN WATTS
LONDON • SYDNEY

CONTENTS

The motorcycle has

been a popular form of transport for more than 100 years. During that time, motorcycles have become increasingly specialised. There are motorcycles for making long-distance journeys and smaller, lightweight machines for making short trips in town. There are sporty superbikes for high-performance fun riding and trail bikes for off-road riding. There are Grand Prix racers for track racing and a variety of motorcycles for different sports such as speedway, ice racing and motocross.

The first motorcycle was made in 1885 from a sturdy wooden frame with a petrol engine under the seat. Small wheels at the sides helped to keep the heavy machine upright.

The Belgian-built *FN* was advanced for its day. Built between 1904 and 1926, it was powered by a four-cylinder engine linked to the rear wheel by a shaft instead of a belt or chain.

The first motorised bicycles were built in the 1860s. They were powered by steam engines but they failed to become popular because they were noisy, smoky and very hot. Then in 1885, a German engineer called Gottlieb Daimler built a bicycle powered by a petrol engine. It was the first practical motorcycle.

Henderson was a make of American motorcycle dating back to 1912.

THE DEVELOPMENT OF THE WHEEL

Wooden wheel

Wire-spoke wheel

Three-spoke wheel

Alloy wheel

The first motorcycle wheels were made from wood. Metal wheels with wire spokes came next. Modern alloy wheels have three strong spokes.

Alfred Scott started making motorcycles in Britain in 1909.

Indian

Indian was a leading early American motorcycle.

BMW has made motorcycles in Germany since 1923.

The modern motorcycle layout, with the engine inside the frame, was adopted quickly by early manufacturers.

The first Harley-Davidson motorcycles used a leather belt to link the engine to the rear wheel. The belt was unreliable and was soon replaced by a chain.

FG 4196

Wire-spoke wheel

A 1914 chain-driven Harley-Davidson

The Zündapp (1932) had a unique pressed steel frame.

The British Vincent Black Shadow (1950s) was very fast.

Japanese motorcycles became popular in the late 1960s.

The motorcycle is a finely

balanced blend of power and weight. The Ducati 851 is more powerful than a family car but only about one-fifth of its weight. This combination gives the 851 incredibly fast acceleration and a top speed of 245 kilometres per hour (kph). It is great to ride and is also a successful racing bike.

The Ducati 851's strength lies in the steel framework. The ladder-like frame, called a chassis, is made from steel tubes. The engine itself forms part of this frame.

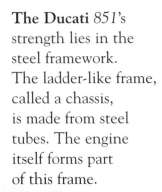

Seat

The Ducati 851 is powered by a type of engine called a V-twin. It has two cylinders at an angle to each other forming a 'V' shape. Each cylinder has four valves to let air in and exhaust gases out.

Exhaust pipe

The rear wheel is attached to an arm that can swing up and down to absorb bumps in the road, making the ride smoother.

Italian motorcycles are often painted red because that is Italy's racing colour. This Ducati is from Italy.

Fuel tank   *Chassis*

Throttle control

A sleek, streamlined fairing is wrapped around the engine. This enables air to flow smoothly around it and reduce air resistance that would slow the bike.

Fairing

Front Brake

Engine

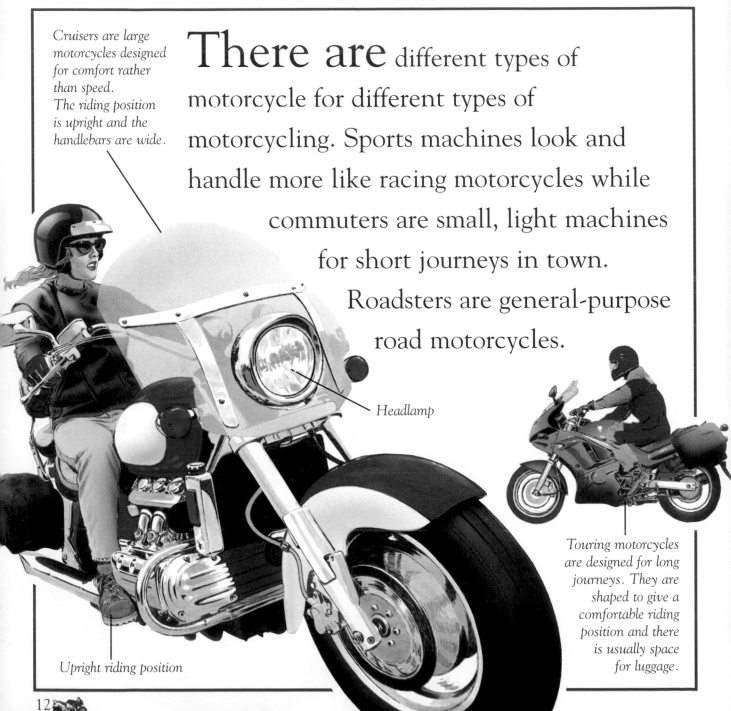

Cruisers are large motorcycles designed for comfort rather than speed. The riding position is upright and the handlebars are wide.

There are different types of motorcycle for different types of motorcycling. Sports machines look and handle more like racing motorcycles while commuters are small, light machines for short journeys in town. Roadsters are general-purpose road motorcycles.

Headlamp

Upright riding position

Touring motorcycles are designed for long journeys. They are shaped to give a comfortable riding position and there is usually space for luggage.

There are also street copies of off-road trail bikes. Some motorcycles, like the sports tourer, combine the best of two different types of machine.

Sports tourer

The sports tourer is for people who want to make long-distance journeys in comfort, but want a sportier performance than the standard tourer.

Commuter bike

Trail bikes are tall, light motorcycles designed for use on rough ground.

Commuter bikes perform at their best at the lower speeds of town traffic. They are lightweight machines that can turn tightly allowing them to manoeuvre through gaps in traffic.

The wheels move up and down further to absorb the impact of bumpy roads.

The design of a motorcycle is often influenced by the country where it is manufactured. Countries with long distances between towns are known for touring motorcycles. Countries with a flair for design produce the most stylish machines.

Britain's motorcycle industry was wiped out in the 1960s by the arrival of superior Japanese motorcycles. Triumph is one of the few British names to survive.

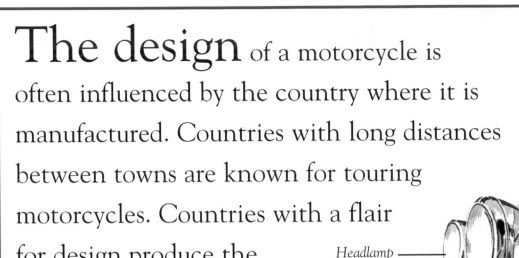

Windscreen

Headlamp

Chrome fittings

Triumph Daytona

Harley-Davidson Heritage
Softail Classic FLSTN

V-twin engine   Exhaust-pipe   Saddle-bag

With its wide, open spaces
and extensive road network,
the USA is famous for large,
powerful, comfortable
motorcycles such as those
built by Harley-Davidson.

Germany is renowned for making
large touring motorcycles like this
BMW.

Italian designers create stylish
sports motorcycles like this
Ducati 748.

Japan supplies almost every
type of motorcycle to the rest
of the world. This is a Honda
CBR 600F.

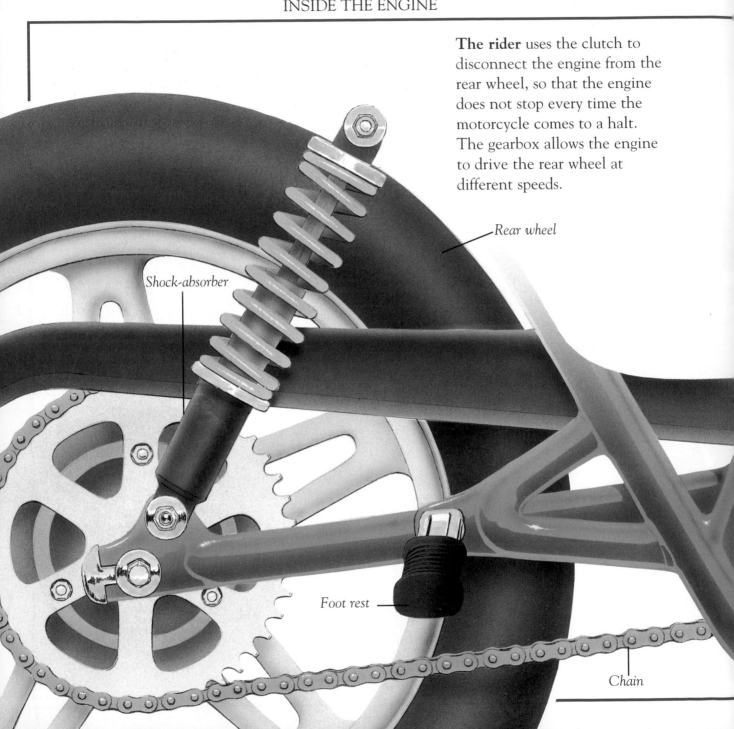

The rider uses the clutch to disconnect the engine from the rear wheel, so that the engine does not stop every time the motorcycle comes to a halt. The gearbox allows the engine to drive the rear wheel at different speeds.

Rear wheel

Shock-absorber

Foot rest

Chain

Motorcycles are powered by piston engines. Petrol burned inside one or more cylinders moves pistons which turn a main shaft called a crankshaft. A chain or belt transfers the engine power to the rear wheel.

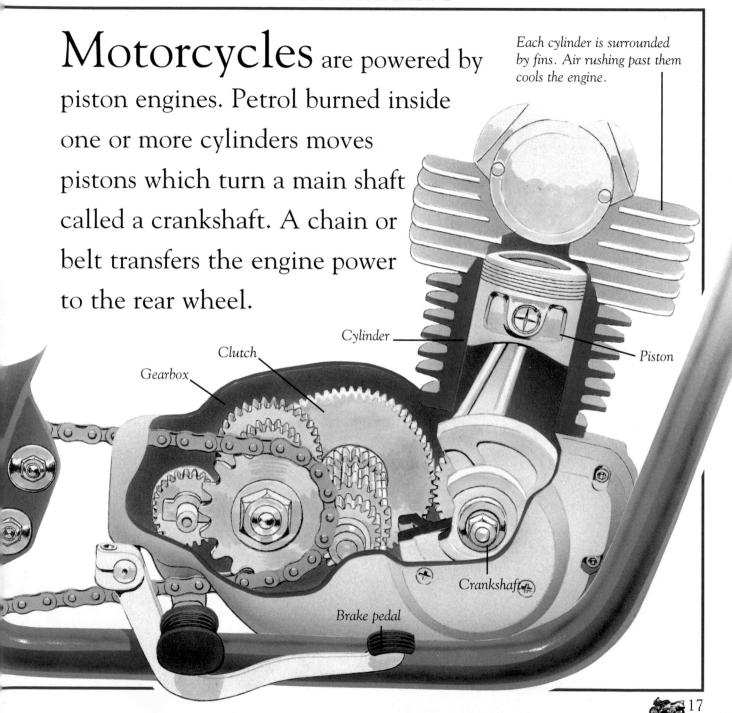

Each cylinder is surrounded by fins. Air rushing past them cools the engine.

Cylinder

Piston

Clutch

Gearbox

Crankshaft

Brake pedal

A control panel gives the rider important information about the motorcycle. The speedometer shows how fast it is going. The odometer shows how far it has travelled since it was made and the tripmeter shows how far it travels on each journey. The rev counter shows the engine speed, and there is also an engine temperature gauge. Switches on the handlebars control the lights, direction indicators and horn. The rider controls engine speed by twisting the right hand-grip. The clutch and front brake are also operated by the hands, while the feet select the gears and operate the rear brake.

Light

The clutch lever disconnects the engine from the wheels while changing gear or stopping.

Hand-grip

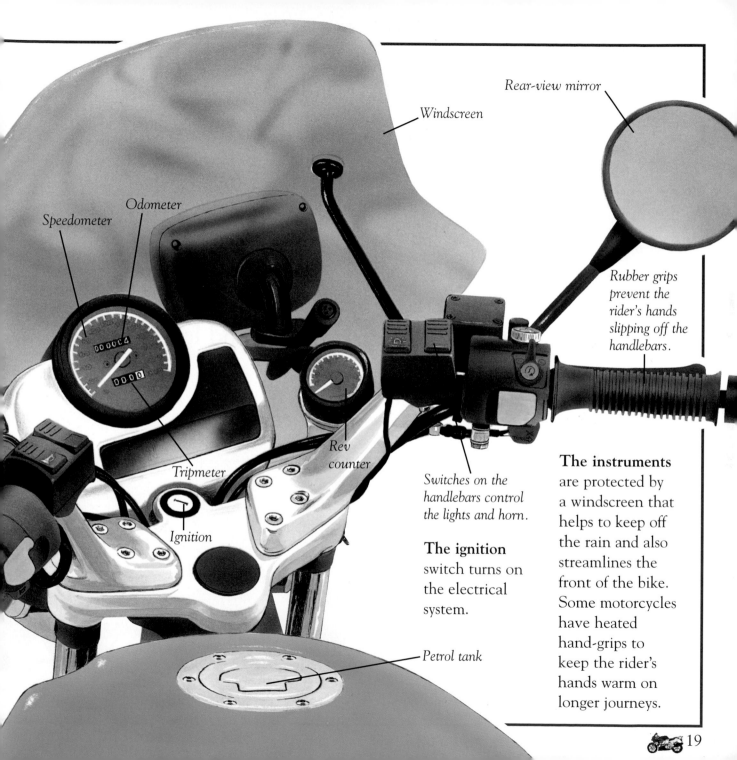

Rear-view mirror

Windscreen

Speedometer

Odometer

00 000 4

0000

Tripmeter

Ignition

Rev
counter

Rubber grips
prevent the
rider's hands
slipping off the
handlebars.

Switches on the
handlebars control
the lights and horn.

The ignition
switch turns on
the electrical
system.

Petrol tank

The instruments
are protected by
a windscreen that
helps to keep off
the rain and also
streamlines the
front of the bike.
Some motorcycles
have heated
hand-grips to
keep the rider's
hands warm on
longer journeys.

Army motorcycle riders were often the only means of communication when telephone and radio links broke down.

BMW R75

The most famous motorcycle used by the German army in World War II was the BMW *R75*. It was usually fitted with a side-car and could reach 95 kilometres per hour.

Motorcycles were used in wartime because of their speed, small size and manoeuvrability. Important messages were carried by dispatch riders in both world wars. Motorcycles were also used for reconnaissance – scouting around the countryside and locating the enemy.

About 80,000 Harley-Davidson WLA 45's (right) were made for military service during World War II. They were used by the American, British and Russian armies.

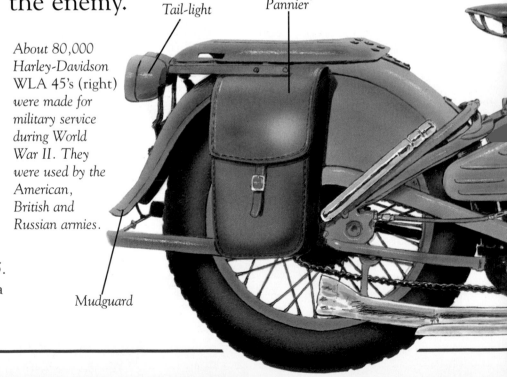

Tail-light

Pannier

Mudguard

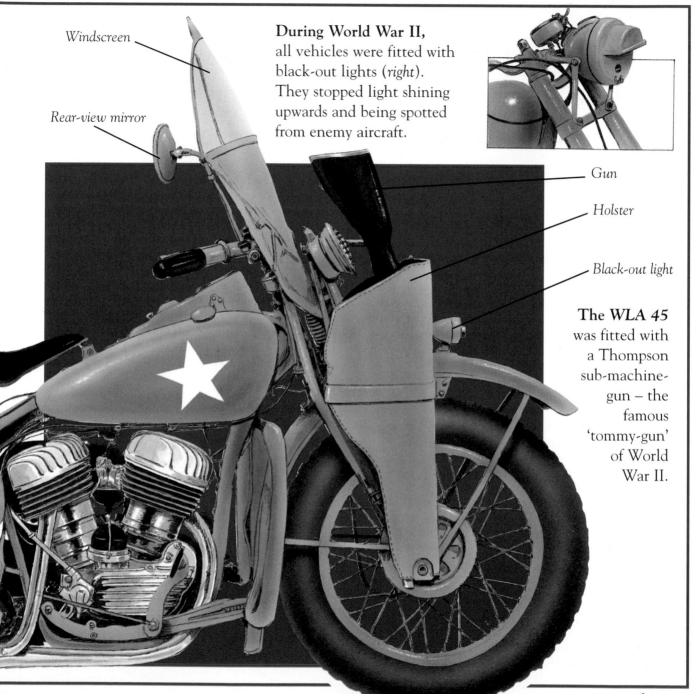

Windscreen

Rear-view mirror

During World War II, all vehicles were fitted with black-out lights (*right*). They stopped light shining upwards and being spotted from enemy aircraft.

Gun

Holster

Black-out light

The WLA 45 was fitted with a Thompson sub-machine-gun – the famous 'tommy-gun' of World War II.

In an emergency, it is important that people skilled in medical care or law enforcement reach the scene of the emergency as quickly as possible. Heavy traffic in busy towns slows down cars and ambulances, but motorcycles can get through much more quickly and easily. Police forces and paramedics (people trained to give emergency medical aid) often use specially adapted motorcycles for this work.

A paramedic on a motorcycle rushes to the scene of an accident. Information about the accident and its location is sent to the rider by radio. A siren sounds and lights flash to warn other vehicles to move out of the way and let the motorcycle through. Luggage-carriers on either side of the back wheel contain essential medical equipment.

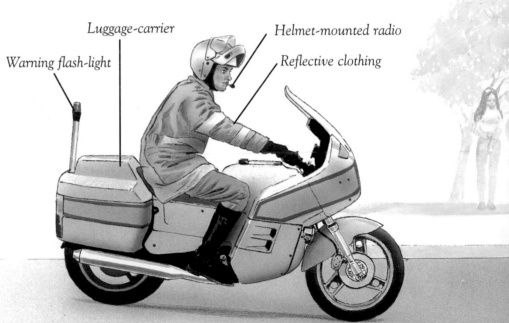

Luggage-carrier

Warning flash-light

Helmet-mounted radio

Reflective clothing

Honda produces a modified version of its ST1100 motorcycle for police forces.

Harley-Davidsons have been popular with American police forces for decades.

Specially modified BMW motorcycles are popular with European police forces.

Some American state police forces began to use Japanese Kawasaki motorcycles in the 1980s.

A fleet of motorcycles cruise the streets of Paris, France, cleaning up after the city's two million pet dogs. Each motorcycle is equipped with a powerful vacuum cleaner, and a tank to hold dogs' dirt.

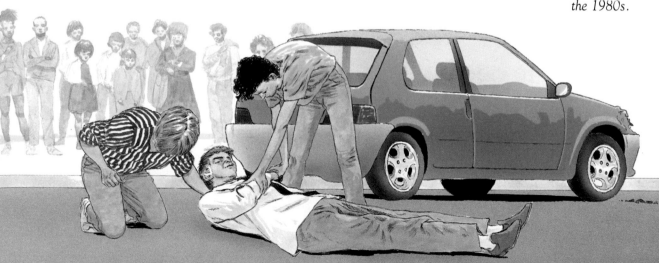

Off-road sports require very tough and agile motorcycles to cope with bumpy, loose surfaces. Motocross involves racing around a muddy course. Desert races are held in the sands of the Sahara and other deserts. Enduro riders have to reach check-points at set times and then complete tasks such as wheel changes.

Motocross riders

Riders jostle for position as they lean their racing machines over to take a corner. The soft, sticky rubber of the tyres grips the track surface and stops the wheels from sliding out.

Racing motorcycles are

divided into different classes. This is usually done according to their engine size to ensure that races are exciting contests between closely matched machines. Most races are held over a certain number of laps of a circuit and the winner is the first rider to cross the finish line. Endurance races are won by completing the greatest distance in a certain time – usually 24 hours.

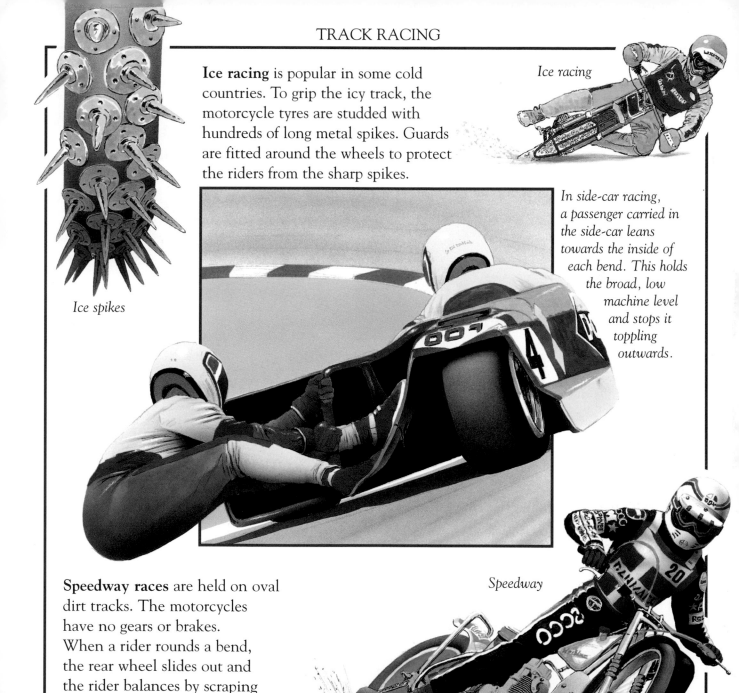

Ice racing is popular in some cold countries. To grip the icy track, the motorcycle tyres are studded with hundreds of long metal spikes. Guards are fitted around the wheels to protect the riders from the sharp spikes.

Ice racing

Ice spikes

In side-car racing, a passenger carried in the side-car leans towards the inside of each bend. This holds the broad, low machine level and stops it toppling outwards.

Speedway races are held on oval dirt tracks. The motorcycles have no gears or brakes. When a rider rounds a bend, the rear wheel slides out and the rider balances by scraping one foot along the ground.

Speedway

27

Two riders crouch low over their dragsters while they wait for the start signal. The signal to go is shown on a tower of lights called a Christmas tree. When the lights change from red to green, the riders set off down the drag strip. A barrier between the lanes stops the bikes colliding.

Dragsters are motorcycles designed to reach the maximum possible speed in a straight line. They race on a 402-metre long straight track called a drag strip. Dragsters always race in pairs. Two machines hurtle down the drag strip, each straining to reach the finish line first. The winning dragster can be travelling at over 350 kilometres per hour when it crosses the line.

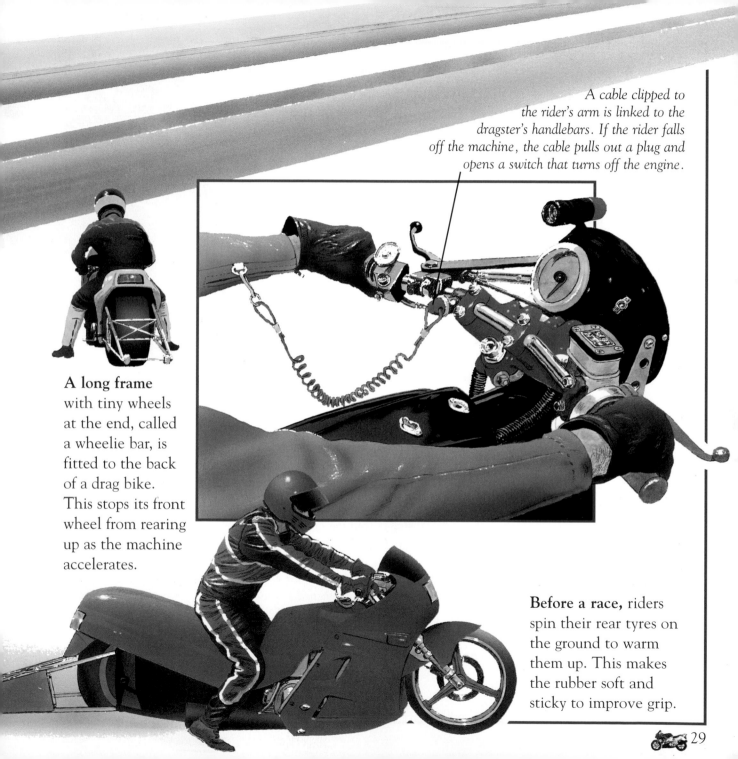

A cable clipped to the rider's arm is linked to the dragster's handlebars. If the rider falls off the machine, the cable pulls out a plug and opens a switch that turns off the engine.

A long frame with tiny wheels at the end, called a wheelie bar, is fitted to the back of a drag bike. This stops its front wheel from rearing up as the machine accelerates.

Before a race, riders spin their rear tyres on the ground to warm them up. This makes the rubber soft and sticky to improve grip.

Safety begins with the rider's clothing. A helmet is essential to protect the rider's head. Tough, padded clothes are specially made for motorcyclists to provide the maximum protection in an accident, without making it too difficult to move. Some riders wear body armour or spine protectors for extra protection. Bright colours and reflective patches on clothing make riders easier to see on the road.

Most motorcyclists wear a helmet that protects the whole head. It is held in place by a strap underneath the chin.

Helmet

Waterproof jacket

Thick gloves

Waterproof trousers with knee-pads

Clothing made specially for motorcyclists keeps out the rain and cold, and also helps to protect the rider from injury in the event of an accident. Strengthened elbow- and knee-pads give the joints extra protection. Sturdy boots provide firm support for the ankles and help protect the toes and shins.

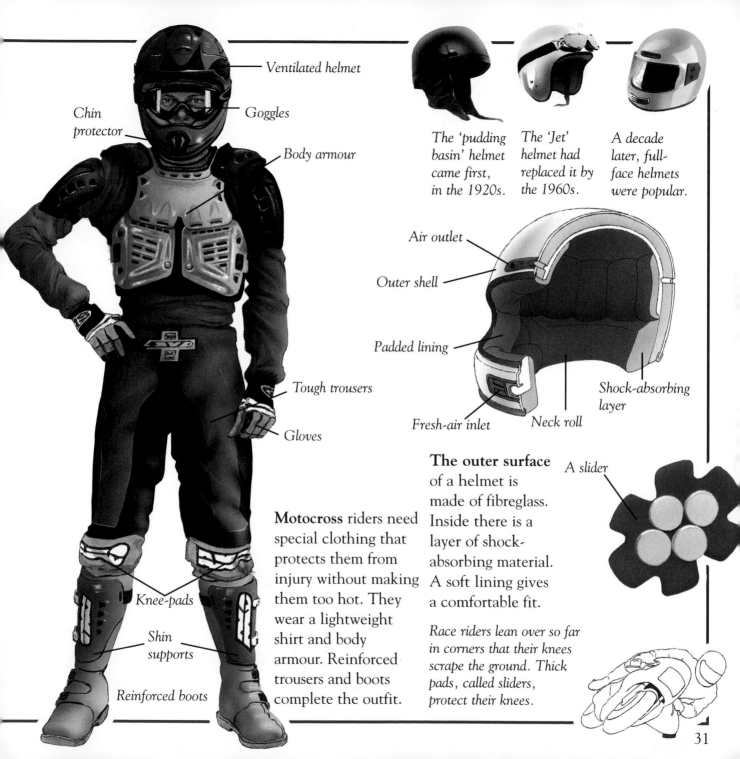

Ventilated helmet

Chin protector

Goggles

Body armour

Tough trousers

Gloves

Knee-pads

Shin supports

Reinforced boots

The 'pudding basin' helmet came first, in the 1920s.

The 'Jet' helmet had replaced it by the 1960s.

A decade later, full-face helmets were popular.

Air outlet

Outer shell

Padded lining

Shock-absorbing layer

Fresh-air inlet

Neck roll

Motocross riders need special clothing that protects them from injury without making them too hot. They wear a lightweight shirt and body armour. Reinforced trousers and boots complete the outfit.

The outer surface of a helmet is made of fibreglass. Inside there is a layer of shock-absorbing material. A soft lining gives a comfortable fit.

A slider

Race riders lean over so far in corners that their knees scrape the ground. Thick pads, called sliders, protect their knees.

31

Superbikes are fast, powerful, high performance road-going motorcycles.

They are also a popular class of racing motorcycle. The machines that take part in superbike racing have to be very similar to standard road models. This makes superbike racing far less expensive than many other forms of motorcycle sport. It also makes superbikes very popular with racing fans because they can ride a motorcycle on the road that looks like the motorcycles they see competing on the racetrack.

Honda's *CBR1100xx Super Blackbird* (right) is one of world's biggest and most powerful superbikes. It is also the most streamlined. Its specially designed bullet-shaped nose is the perfect shape for cutting through air. A four-cylinder engine supplies as much power as any motorcyclist could want. The engine needs extra cooling so specially shaped slots in the fairing draw through air to stop the engine overheating.

Ducati motorcycles are known for their stylish good looks and sporty performance. The Ducati 916 is often described as the most beautiful road-going motorcycle ever made.

Ducati 916

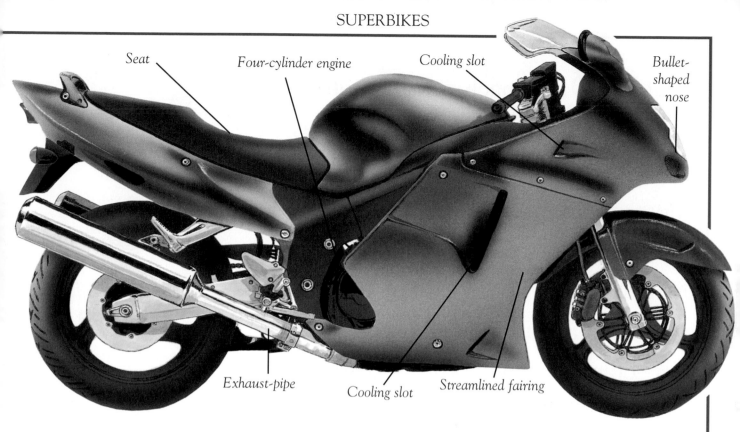

Seat

Four-cylinder engine

Cooling slot

Bullet-shaped nose

Exhaust-pipe

Cooling slot

Streamlined fairing

The Honda Fireblade is one of the world's most desirable road-going superbikes. A 900cc four-cylinder engine gives the Fireblade a top speed of 260 kilometres per hour.

Suzuki's GSX-R750 was one of the first road-going superbikes that was styled to look like a racing machine. It has become one of the world's best-selling superbikes.

Honda Fireblade

Suzuki GSX-R750

Custom machines are motorcycles that have been changed in some way to make them look different from other motorcycles. Some customisers give an existing motorcycle a wild paint scheme or rebuild it with shiny chrome parts. Others start with an engine and chassis and build a spectacular new motorcycle from scratch.

The distinctive Harley-Davidson badge, and eagle emblem.

This custom three-wheeler (*left*) was built from a Mercedes-Benz car engine with parts from Jaguar and Porsche cars, and Harley-Davidson motorcycles.

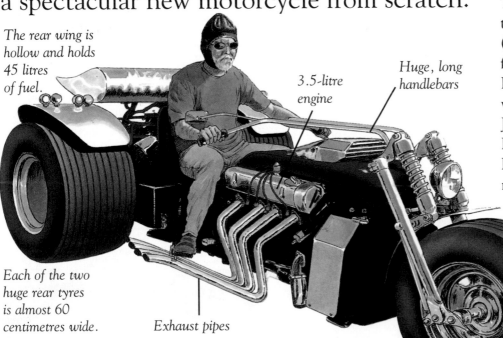

The rear wing is hollow and holds 45 litres of fuel.

3.5-litre engine

Huge, long handlebars

Each of the two huge rear tyres is almost 60 centimetres wide.

Exhaust pipes

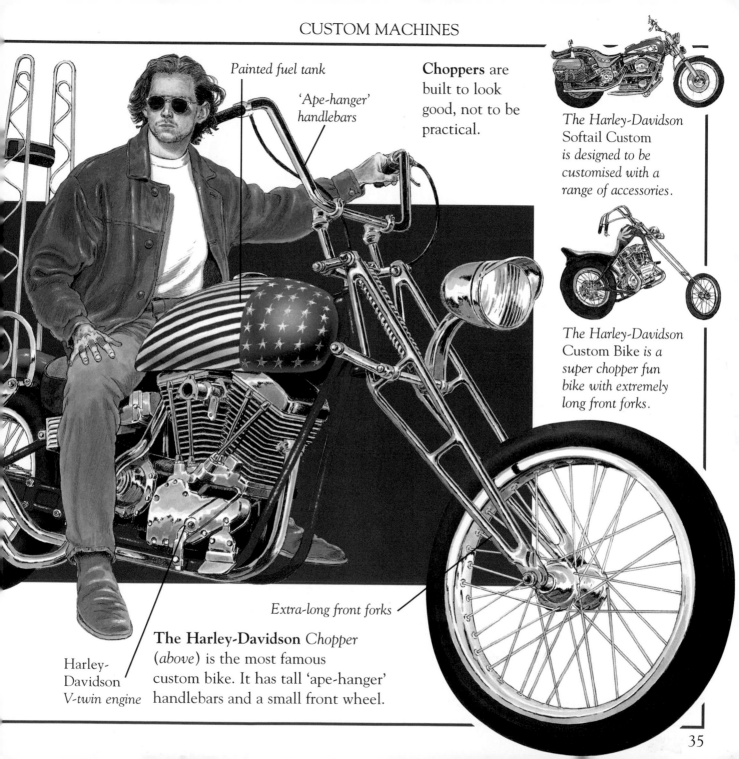

Painted fuel tank

'Ape-hanger' handlebars

Choppers are built to look good, not to be practical.

The Harley-Davidson Softail Custom *is designed to be customised with a range of accessories.*

The Harley-Davidson Custom Bike *is a super chopper fun bike with extremely long front forks.*

Extra-long front forks

The Harley-Davidson *Chopper* (*above*) is the most famous custom bike. It has tall 'ape-hanger' handlebars and a small front wheel.

Harley-Davidson *V-twin engine*

When this Temple-Anzani motorcycle (left) set a new record of 174 kilometres per hour (kph) in 1923 at the Brooklands racetrack in England, designers did not yet understand the importance of streamlining.

This Triumph (below) reached a speed of 345 kph in 1956. The rider lies back in the cramped cockpit.

By the 1950s, record-breaking motorcycles were being built in the shape of a long, narrow streamlined tube to reduce air resistance.

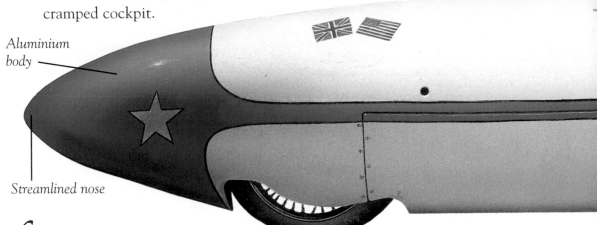

Aluminium body

Streamlined nose

The first speed records were set on roads and racetracks, but as speeds increased, record attempts needed more space. Record challengers moved to Daytona Beach in Florida, USA. Then in the 1950s it was the turn of the Bonneville Salt Flats in Utah, USA.

The current record of 518 kilometres per
hour was set there by Dave Campos in 1990.
He rode a torpedo-shaped machine powered
by two Harley-Davidson engines.

*The world's first
racetrack was
opened at
Brooklands in
Surrey, England,
in 1907.*

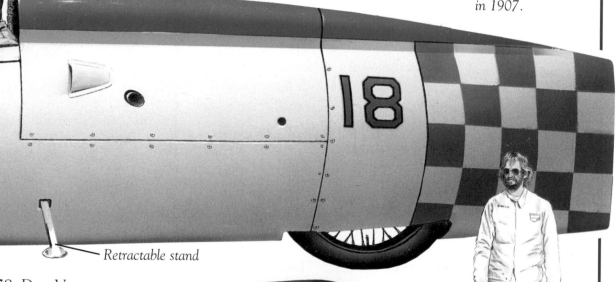

Retractable stand

In 1978, Don Vesco
set a new record speed
of 512 kph on the
Bonneville Salt Flats in
his motorcycle *Lightning
Bolt*. The streamlined
machine was powered by
two 1,000cc Kawasaki
motorcycle engines.

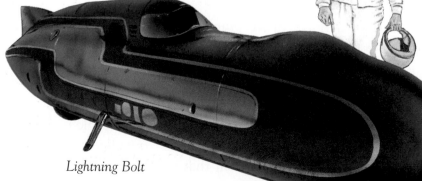

Lightning Bolt

37

USEFUL WORDS

Chassis A motorcycle's main frame.

Clutch Control used to disconnect the engine from the rear wheel while stopping or changing gear.

Commuter A lightweight motorcycle for short journeys in town.

Cruiser A type of motorcycle built for comfort and style.

Cylinder Where the fuel is burned inside an engine.

Dragster A motorcycle designed to travel as fast as possible in a straight line down a drag strip.

Fairing The smoothly curving cover fitted round a motorcycle.

Odometer An instrument that shows the total distance travelled.

Rev counter An instrument that shows the engine speed.

Sliders Tough pads to protect a race rider's knees.

Spark-plug The part of an engine that produces the electric spark to burn the fuel.

Speedometer The instrument that shows a motorcycle's speed.

Throttle The twist-grip control that changes the engine speed.

Tourer A motorcycle designed for comfort on long journeys.

Trail bike A lightweight motorcycle for off-road riding.

Tread Grooves cut into a tyre to improve grip.

Tripmeter An instrument that shows how far a motorcycle has travelled on its latest journey.

INDEX